The Mini Page ®

Guide to the
Constitution

★ ★ ★ ★ ★ ★ ★ ★ ★ ★ ★ ★ ★

By BETTY DEBNAM

In Collaboration with the National Archives

Andrews McMeel
Publishing, LLC

Kansas City

Contents

By BETTY DEBNAM

You have something in common with all these U.S. citizens … and millions of others who are alive today or who have lived in the past.

Famous people…

    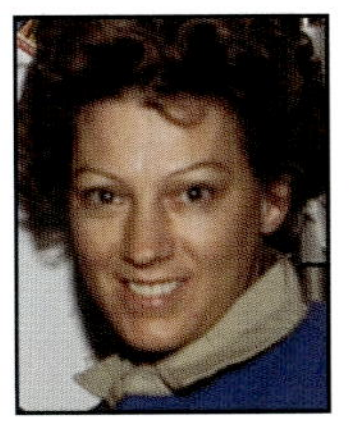  

Kids just like you…

 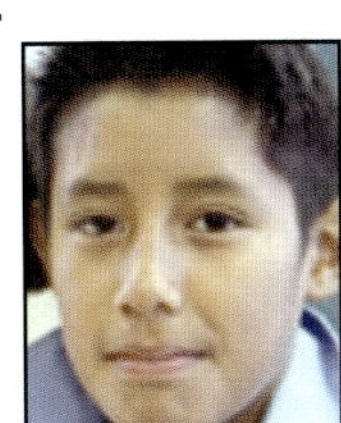  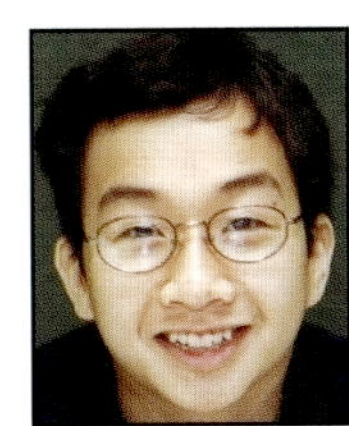 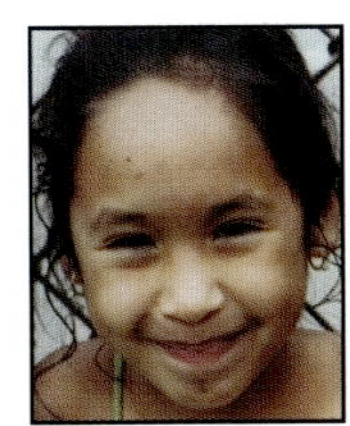 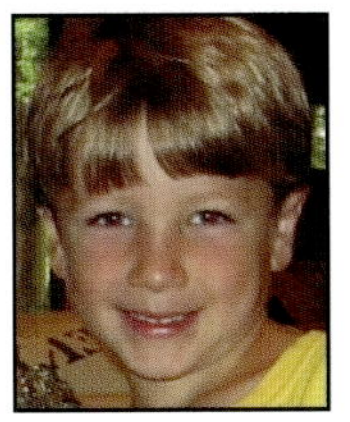 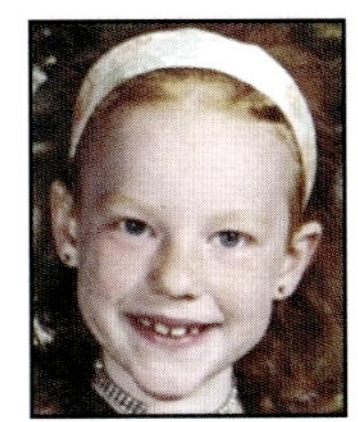

Our Constitution

The Constitution is the supreme law of the land. It is a set of basic laws organizing, granting and limiting the powers of our government. It is something that we all share.

The Constitution is handwritten on four parchment pages. Each page is about 29 inches high and 24 inches wide.

Basic facts

- It was created in Philadelphia…
- during the summer of 1787…
- in secret…
- in 87 days.
- It has 39 signers…
- and is made up of a preamble, seven articles, and 27 amendments added later.

We thank the staff of the National Archives, and Lee Ann Potter, director of education and volunteer programs, for their help.
Site to see:
www.archives.gov

The Constitution is on display at the National Archives building in Washington, D.C. An archives is a place where important documents are preserved.

Famous people in Row 1 (left to right): George Washington, Laura Bush, Martin Luther King Jr., Eleanor Roosevelt, astronaut Eileen Collins, Abraham Lincoln, Oprah Winfrey.

from The Mini Page by Betty Debnam © 2005 The Mini Page Publishing Company Inc.

Mini Constitution Guide

What's the big idea?

U.S. Capitol

LEGISLATIVE BRANCH

White House

EXECUTIVE BRANCH

Supreme Court

JUDICIAL BRANCH

Inside the Constitution are several big ideas:

• **Separation of powers:** The delegates feared that giving too much power to any person or group could be dangerous. So they created three branches, or parts, of government: executive, legislative and judicial.

• **Checks and balances:** This limits the power of each government branch. No single branch can overpower the others. Often, each branch needs the help of the others to do its job.

• **Enumerated (e-NOOM-er-ate-ed) powers:** the listed powers of government.

• **Implied powers:** the powers that are not listed but suggested.

• **Federalism:** the idea that our government divides powers between the national government and the state governments.

We will have more about the big ideas in the issues to come.

The Constitution has:

• A preamble (an introduction)
• Seven articles (sections) covering:

Article I: The Congress (legislative branch)

Article II: The president (executive branch)

Article III: The judges and national courts (judicial branch)

Article IV: How states relate to each other and the national government.

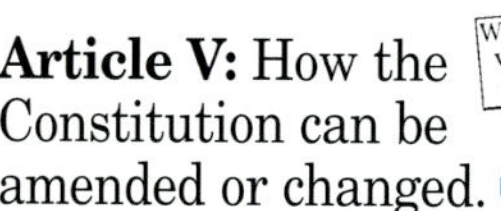

Article V: How the Constitution can be amended or changed.

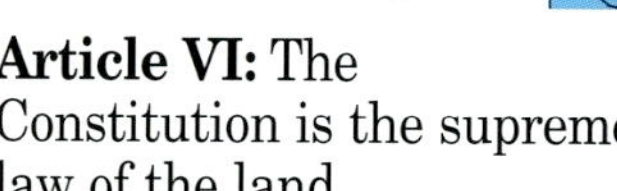

Article VI: The Constitution is the supreme law of the land.

Article VII: Ratification, or approval.

• The signatures of 39 delegates.

Amendments to the Constitution

Our Constitution is not perfect. It has been amended, or changed. Twenty-seven amendments have been added. The first 10 are called the Bill of Rights (1791).

1st: freedom of religion

freedom of speech

freedom of the press

freedom of assembly and petition.

2nd: right to bear arms.

3rd: quartering of soldiers limited.

4th: searches and seizures regulated.

5th: rights to due process of law, including protection against self-incrimination.

6th: rights of a person accused of a crime, including the right to be represented by a lawyer.

7th: right to a trial by jury.

8th: unfair bail, fines and punishment forbidden.

9th: citizens entitled to rights not listed in the Constitution.

10th: powers not listed reserved to the states or the people.

11th: rules for lawsuits against states (1795).

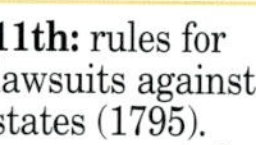

12th: new way of selecting the president and vice president. (1804)

13th: slavery abolished (1865).

14th: rights of citizenship, due process and equal protection under the law (1868).

15th: voting rights for former slaves (1870).

16th: federal income taxes authorized (1913).

17th: U.S. senators to be elected by the people (1913).

18th: sale of alcohol banned (1919).

19th: women gained right to vote (1920).

20th: dates of the presidential and congressional terms set (1933).

21st: 18th Amendment repealed (1933).

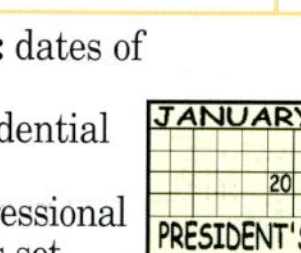

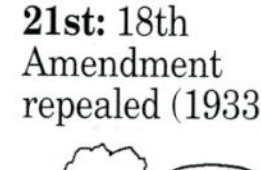

22nd: president limited to two terms (1951).

23rd: people in District of Columbia given right to vote for president (1961).

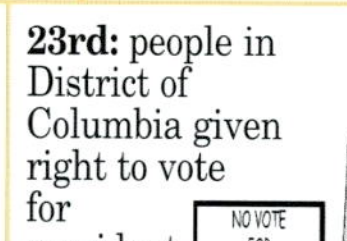

24th: no poll taxes in federal elections (1964).

25th: presidential succession and disability (1967).

26th: voting age lowered to 18 (1971).

27th: congressional salaries regulated (1992).

from The Mini Page by Betty Debnam © 2005 The Mini Page Publishing Company Inc.

Would You Like to See the Real Thing?

A mother and her daughter examine the original Constitution in the Rotunda, a huge room in the National Archives.

photos courtesy National Archives

Our country's most valuable charters, or documents, are displayed in special cases under special glass. Visiting the National Archives, you can see:
1. The Declaration of Independence;
2. All four pages of the Constitution; and
3. The Bill of Rights.

photo by Carol Highsmith

Some of the million people who come to see the original Constitution every year sign a guest book and make comments. Here are a few:

"I like the Constitution. I am impressed that it is still around."
— Anonymous

"We didn't realize they used such big paper."
— Amanda from New York

"Kudos to the Founding Fathers for being so awesome."
— Anonymous

"When we saw the phrase, 'We the people' on the Constitution, I felt so proud. I thought this was so cool!"
— Shelby from California

"I've always heard about this place in my class."
— Mika from Japan

"I think every kid in America should read these and see the documents in real life."
— Anonymous

"Even though we are not Americans, this was an amazing experience."
— three girls from Germany

---

from The Mini Page by Betty Debnam © 2005 The Mini Page Publishing Company Inc.

Mini Spy ...

Mini Spy and her friends are visiting the Constitution and Declaration of Independence at the National Archives. See if you can find: • man in the moon • two mushrooms

- ladder • ruler
- bird • key
- number 3
- letter E • olive
- heart • teapot
- carrot • tooth
- question mark
- paperclip
- toothbrush
- pencil • bell
- exclamation point
- word MINI

---

from The Mini Page by Betty Debnam © 2005 The Mini Page Publishing Company Inc.

Basset Brown The News Hound's CONSTITUTION TRY 'N FIND

Words and names that remind us of the Constitution are hidden in the block below. Some words are hidden backward or diagonally, and some letters are used twice. See if you can find: SUPREME, COURT, PHILADELPHIA, ARTICLES, NATIONAL, ARCHIVES, HANDWRITTEN, PARCHMENT, PRESIDENT, UNITED, STATES, AMENDMENT, WASHINGTON, LAWS, GOVERNMENT.

```
Z K A R T I C L E S B F T X T
V J L A N O I T A N O S N K N
N O T G N I H S A W Q P E S E
G O V E R N M E N T S J M U M
Y O A I H P L E D A L I H P D
S E T A T S D E T I N U C R N
F A R C H I V E S V G B R E E
L N E T T I R W D N A H A M M
C O U R T N E D I S E R P E A
```

By BETTY DEBNAM

The Preamble

Our Constitution's Purpose

Most people agree that these first three words – "We the People" – are the most important words in the Constitution. They clearly say that the American people are in charge of their government. This is known as "popular sovereignty." The people hold the power.

Who are "We the People"?

In 1787, when the Constitution was written, there were almost 4 million people in the United States.

Today there are about 300 million. We the people have grown!

George Washington served as president of the Constitutional Convention. While the Constitution was being worked out, he had a printed copy of what was being considered. In this draft, the original 13 states were listed right after "We the People."

WE the People of the States of New-Hampshire, Massachusetts, Rhode-Island and Providence Plantations, Connecticut, New-York, New-Jersey, Pennsylvania, Delaware, Maryland, Virginia, North-Carolina, South-Carolina, and Georgia, do ordain, declare and establish the following Constitution for the Government of Ourselves and our Posterity.

The above is only the top of George Washington's first page. Can you read the original states?

The Preamble set forth six goals for our government:

(1) In order to form a more perfect union ... The union of the states under the first laws of the land, the Articles of Confederation, were just not working. There were many problems.

(2) Establish justice ... The laws of the land had to be fair to all citizens.

(3) Insure domestic tranquility (to promise peace within the country) ... The states had been quarreling among themselves.

(4) Provide for the common defense ... During the Revolutionary War, the states found out how hard it was to raise money and troops. Strong national forces would make a stronger country.

(5) Promote the general welfare ... State governments needed to work together for the well-being of all citizens.

(6) And secure the blessings of liberty for ourselves and our posterity (descendants) ... **do ordain and establish** (set up) **this Constitution for the United States of America.**

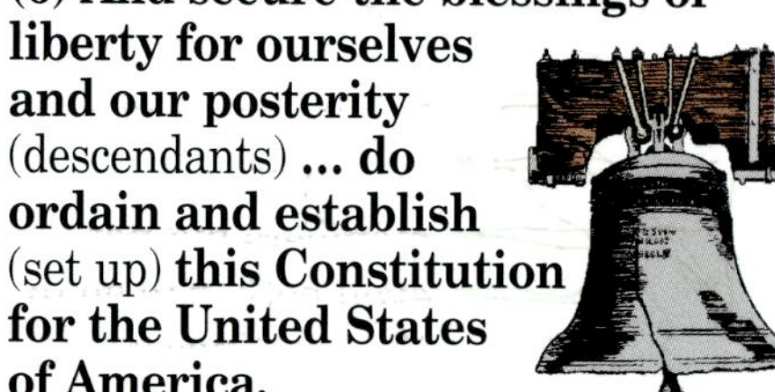

Our First Laws Were Weak

from The Mini Page by Betty Debnam © 2005 The Mini Page Publishing Company Inc.

An artist's idea of weary soldiers and Gen. Washington at Valley Forge, Pa., in the winter of 1777-1778 during the Revolution. Things were so bad that this was called "the winter of despair."

The Articles of Confederation

The Articles of Confederation were our new country's first laws.

A "confederation" is a group united together for a purpose. The Articles of Confederation joined our original 13 states.

The Articles held our country together during the fight for independence.

When the American Revolution was over and the enemy threat was gone, the states became interested only in themselves.

There were many problems because there was no strong central government.

Other countries had no respect for us: Our government was so weak that England kept some of the forts it agreed to give up after the Revolutionary War.

Committees ran the central government, but they had little power. Many members did not even bother to go to the meetings.

Taxes: The government did not have the power to collect taxes. George Washington was well aware of this problem. During the Revolutionary War, many troops were ragged and hungry. Some troops paid for their own gunpowder.

Trade: The government had no powers over trade or commerce. Dealing with other countries was hard because Congress could not speak for all states. States even set tariffs, or taxes, on items coming in from other states.

You might have heard the expression, "It's not worth a Continental." This can be traced back to money issued by the Continental Congress.

Money: The government had no control over paper money. Each state could print its own.

Meeting at Mount Vernon, 1785

The meeting at Mount Vernon was called the Mount Vernon Conference. George Washington invited the delegates to meet there.

After the Revolution, the government of the 13 states was not strong enough to straighten out differences between the states.

The purpose of this meeting was to settle differences between Maryland and Virginia. The five delegates settled the differences, and then decided to hold a meeting once a year and invite all 13 states.

Meeting at Annapolis, 1786

The Annapolis Convention was held at a place called Mann's Tavern.

Five states sent a total of 12 delegates. They took a strong step. They sent word to the Congress and other states that another meeting should be held the next year to rewrite the Articles of Confederation. The meeting in 1787 did more than that. It wrote the Constitution.

We thank the staff of the National Archives, and Lee Ann Potter, director of education and volunteer programs, for their help.

Constitutional Timeline

1776, July 4: Declaration of Independence approved by the Continental Congress.

1781, March 1: Thirteen states ratify the Articles of Confederation, our country's first Constitution.

1783, Sept. 3: Treaty of Paris that ends the Revolutionary War is signed.

1785, March 24-28: Mount Vernon Conference marks first time states meet to discuss problems.

1786, Sept. 11-14: Annapolis Convention: Delegates from several states meet and agree that the government must be changed.

1787, May 25: Meeting to write a new Constitution begins in Philadelphia.

1787, Sept. 17: The Constitution is signed by 39 delegates.

1787, Dec. 7: Delaware becomes the first state to ratify the Constitution.

1788, June 21: The Constitution becomes the law of the land when New Hampshire becomes the ninth state to ratify it.

1789, April 30: George Washington becomes the first president of the new United States.

Fall 1789: The Bill of Rights is sent to the states for ratification.

Amendment I:

Congress shall make no law respecting an …

1791, Dec. 15: The Bill of Rights is ratified.

Mini Spy ...

Mini Spy and her friends are marching as Colonial soldiers. See if you can find: • exclamation mark • kite
• ladder
• number 3
• bell • heart
• rowboat
• coffee cup
• feather
• word MINI
• lima bean
• safety pin
• pencil
• pig's face
• letter u

Basset Brown The News Hound's

PREAMBLE

TRY 'N FIND

Words and names that remind us of the Preamble to the Constitution are hidden in the block below. Some words are hidden backward or diagonally, and some letters are used twice. See if you can find: STATES, CONSTITUTION, RIGHTS, POWERS, TRANQUILITY, SOVEREIGNTY, WELFARE, POPULAR, DOMESTIC, GOVERNMENT, UNITED, JUSTICE, LIBERTY, BLESSINGS, POSTERITY.

The Mini Page

By BETTY DEBNAM

Separation of Powers and Compromise
Big Ideas in the Constitution

Separation of powers

The men who wrote our Constitution knew they wanted a strong national government.

The government under the Articles of Confederation just did not work.

The delegates feared that giving too much power to any one person or group could be dangerous.

The delegates decided that the powers of government should be divided. This idea is called separation of powers.

The Legislative Branch is Congress. Congress makes laws, imposes taxes and borrows money.

The Executive Branch is headed by the president. The president has many jobs. One is to see that the laws are carried out.

The Judicial Branch is headed by the Supreme Court, which decides whether the laws passed by Congress are in keeping with the Constitution.

Today our U.S. Congress meets in the Capitol building in Washington, D.C. From this view, the House of Representatives is on the left side and the Senate is on the right. Only a few members have offices in the Capitol. Most have offices in nearby buildings.

Compromise

When the delegates disagreed, they worked out a compromise.

How was the new Congress to be set up? How many members could each state send to Congress? These were the big questions. It was a debate between big and small states.

Virginia Plan

Virginia was a big state. The Virginians suggested that the number of members be decided by the number of people who lived in the state.

James Madison wrote the Virginia Plan.

New Jersey Plan

A smaller state, New Jersey, suggested that all states, big and small, have the same number of members.

William Paterson wrote the New Jersey Plan.

Connecticut Plan

Connecticut came up with what is called "The Great Compromise."

Roger Sherman wrote this plan.

The Great Compromise

This plan set up two lawmaking groups, or "houses," as they are called.

The House of Representatives was to be based on the number of people living in each state.

The other house, called the Senate, was to have the same number of members (two) from each state. Laws had to be passed by both houses.

The Three-Fifths Compromise determined the number of representatives each state could send to the House, based on the number of slaves in that state. While slaves could not vote, every five slaves were counted as three "other persons."

from The Mini Page by Betty Debnam © 2005 The Mini Page Publishing Company Inc.

Page One of the Constitution

The Constitution was handwritten on only four pages.

In this series, we look at this important document based on how the "articles," or sections, were presented page by page.

This issue is about Page One.

It's in the Constitution … Page One

Page One of the Constitution says that every 10 years a census of our nation's population will be taken. This is to see how many people each state can send to the House of Representatives.

Kids study a census listing from the early 1800s. They are studying our Constitution at a workshop at the National Archives building in Washington, D.C.

Site to see: www.archives.gov

We thank the staff of National Archives and Lee Ann Potter, director of education and volunteer programs, for their help.

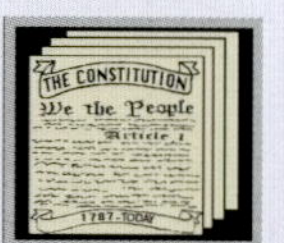

The Preamble

We the People of the United States, in order to form a more perfect union, establish justice, insure domestic tranquility, provide for the common defense, promote the general welfare, and secure the blessings of liberty to ourselves and our posterity, do ordain and establish this Constitution for the United States of America.

Article I
Section I

The Legislative Branch will consist of a Senate and House of Representatives.

Section 2

A member of the House of Representatives:
• must be at least 25 years old.
• must be a citizen of the United States for at least seven years.
• is elected for a two-year term.

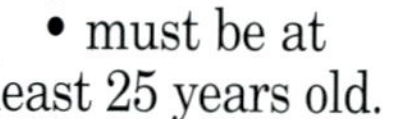

The number of representatives from each state will depend upon how many people live in the state.

The House of Representatives has the sole power to call for an impeachment. (An impeachment occurs when an elected official is charged with misconduct.)

Section 3

A member of the Senate:
• must be at least 30 years old.
• must be a citizen of the United States for at least nine years.
• is elected for a six-year term.

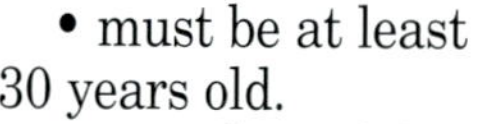

The vice president of the United States is the president of the Senate.

The Senate has the sole power to try all impeachments.

Section 4

This section addresses when elections are to be held and when the Congress shall meet.

Section 5

Deals with the important ways Congress does its business. Each house of Congress can set its own rules. Each house is to keep a journal.

Section 6

Members of Congress are paid by the U.S. government. They are prohibited from serving any other government while in the Congress.

Section 7

Begins on the first page of the Constitution, but most of it is on Page 2. We will learn about that in the next issue in the series.

Engrossing the Constitution

On a separate piece of paper, try to write "We the People" in the same way Jacob Shallus did.

Have you ever heard of Jacob Shallus?

At the time of the convention to write the Constitution, he was an assistant clerk (or secretary) for the Pennsylvania State Assembly, the law-making group for that colony.

After the delegates had agreed on the text of the Constitution, it was carefully copied, or engrossed, on parchment. This version was signed by delegates at the convention.

Careful research has discovered that Jacob Shallus was probably the penman who copied the Constitution.

Although his name does not appear on the document, there is an entry for $30 for "clerks employed to transcribe (or copy) and engross." (When we engross a document, we write it out in large letters.)

While there were printed versions of the Constitution, the engrossed version was the official one.

While there is no record of where Jacob Shallus did the engrossing, it was probably in Independence Hall.

Like many important documents, the Constitution is on parchment. Parchment is made from the skin of animals, especially goats and sheep.

To make parchment, the hair or wool is removed. The skins are placed in a liquid mix that removes the fat. Then the skins are stretched on a frame and scraped.

To soften the skins, powdered chalk is rubbed on with a special stone.

The Constitution was written with a quill and ink. Quills were usually made out of turkey feathers.

Mini Spy ...

Mini Spy and her friends are visiting the Capitol grounds. See if you can find: • question mark • word MINI • banana

- sailboat
- caterpillar
- muffin
- dog's face
- letter A
- man in the moon
- ear of corn
- toothbrush
- man's face
- umbrella
- ladder • book
- number 3
- canoe • heart

Basset Brown The News Hound's Constitution TRY 'N FIND

Words and names that remind us of the Constitution are hidden in the block below. Some words are hidden backward, and some letters are used twice. See if you can find: VOTE, LEGISLATIVE, SENATORS, RULES, UNITED STATES, ELECTIONS, CENSUS, GOVERNMENT, PREAMBLE, HOUSE, DELEGATES, MEMBER, REPRESENTATIVES, MONEY, BILL, ROADS, TAX, QUALIFICATIONS.

```
E V I T A L S I G E L B I L L
R E P R E S E N T A T I V E S
S N O I T A C I F I L A U Q H
E L E C T I O N S Y E N O M O
L S E T A G E L E D V O T E U
U N I T E D S T A T E S Y M S
R O A D S E L B M A E R P B E
W Y S R O T A N E S U S N E C
G O V E R N M E N T A X B R Q
```

By BETTY DEBNAM

from The Mini Page by Betty Debnam © 2005 The Mini Page Publishing Company Inc.

More Big Ideas From Our Constitution
Listed and Suggested Powers

In the last issue of this series, we learned about separation of powers.

We learned that the men who wrote the Constitution were concerned about too much power being in the hands of any one person or part of government.

We learned that the founders created three branches of government. The Constitution gives each branch the power to do different things.

Listed powers

Some of the powers are listed or expressed, or enumerated (e-NOOM-er-ate-ed).

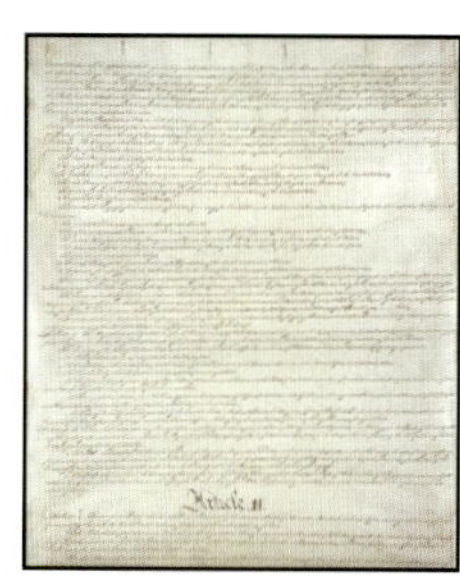

Suggested powers

Some legislative powers are from a part of the Constitution that says that Congress shall make all laws that are "necessary and proper" for carrying out the powers granted by the Constitution.

This is called the "elastic" clause, or part, because it stretches the powers of Congress.

Powers all countries have

There are a few powers that all governments in the world have, so we have them too.

Example: Our national government can make unwanted foreigners leave the country.

Each of these images relates to the listed powers given to Congress on Page 2 of the Constitution. Can you guess what these powers are?

① 

Uncle Sam poster

② 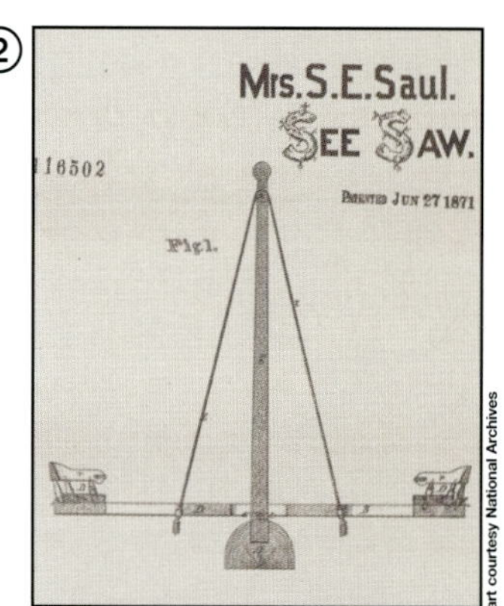

Seesaw patent drawing

③ 

Postal carrier delivering mail

Answers: 1. Congress has the power to "raise and support armies." 2. Congress has the power to "promote the progress of science and the useful arts, by securing ... to authors and inventors the exclusive right to their respective writings and discoveries." 3. Congress has the power to "establish post offices."

from The Mini Page by Betty Debnam © 2005 The Mini Page Publishing Company Inc.

Page Two of the Constitution

Our Constitution was hand-copied, or engrossed, on only four pages.

In our Mini Page series, we are looking at this important document based on how the "articles," or sections, are presented on each page.

In the Constitution ... Page 2

Article 1, Section 8, says: Congress shall have the power to coin money.

The 50 State Quarters Program is the most popular coin program in U.S. history.

For each of the past six years, the part of our government that issues coins, the U.S. Mint, has put out five new state quarters. These coins will never be produced again. The states are honored in the order they were admitted to the union. The program will end in 2009.

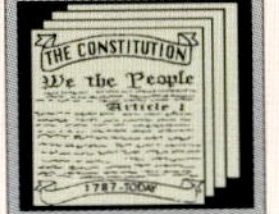

One side of each state quarter will show a fact or event important to that state.

The first state quarter issued in 1999 was that of Delaware, showing Caesar Rodney on horseback dashing from Delaware to sign the Declaration of Independence in 1776 in Philadelphia.

Site to see: www.usmint.gov/kids

We thank the staff of National Archives and Lee Ann Potter, director of education and volunteer programs, for their help.

Remember, our Constitution is only four pages long. The second page has only 1,054 words. It contains the second half of Article I and the beginning of Article II. Article I is about the legislative branch, and Article II is about the executive branch, which we will read about in our next issue.

Article I
Section 7

Explains how a bill becomes a law.

Section 8

Lists the enumerated powers of Congress, including those already presented in this issue, those below and others.

• govern taxes

• declare war

• provide and maintain a navy

Section 9

Lists the limitations on the powers of Congress.

• Forbids Congress from banning importing slaves before 1808.

• Forbids Congress from passing laws that would punish a person without a trial.

• Forbids Congress from granting titles of nobility. (There would be no kings or queens in the United States.)

Article II
Section 1

Begins on this page, but most of it is on Page 3, and we will learn about it in the next issue in this series. It is about the executive branch, or the presidency.

To do: Look through your newspaper for news about what Congress is doing.

The Mini Page is created and edited by
Betty Debnam

Associate Editors
Tali Denton
Lucy Lien

Staff Artist
Wendy Daley

How a Bill Becomes a Law

Understanding the Constitution helps us understand how our government works. One of the most important parts of this is understanding how a bill becomes a law.

1. Proposal:
A bill is proposed in either the House or the Senate and sent to a committee to handle the subject.

2. Committee action:
Since so many bills are proposed, the committee chooses only a few for further study.

3. Debates held:
The House and the Senate discuss the bill, change or amend it, vote on it, and either pass or reject it.

4. Conference committee agrees:
If there is a difference between the bill presented to the House of Representatives and one passed by the Senate, a conference committee works on the differences.

5. The conference report, or rewritten bill, is sent back to the House and the Senate for a "yes" or "no" vote by members.

6. President signs:
The bill is sent to the president for signing. If he vetoes it (doesn't sign), it is sent back to the House and Senate. If it passes again after the veto, with a two-thirds vote in each house, it becomes a law.

Gov. Mike Easley of North Carolina takes the oath of office for his second term in January 2005.

The very first act of Congress, signed into law by President George Washington on June 1, 1789, was "An Act to regulate the Time and Manner of administrating certain Oaths."

The new law required that all members of Congress, all federal officials, all members of state legislatures, judiciaries (court officials) and executives take the simple 14-word oath below.

Officials still take an oath to support the Constitution today.

"I do solemnly swear (or affirm) that I will support the Constitution of the United States."

Mini Spy ...

Mini Spy and her friends collect coins. See if you can find:
• man in the moon • exclamation mark • word MINI • mitten

• sock
• letter D
• kite • letter A
• heart • banana
• toothbrush
• pencil
• bandage
• letter M
• acorn • olive
• snake • letter T
• carrot
• jackknife
• paper clip
• number 8

Basset Brown The News Hound's

Constitution

TRY 'N FIND

Words that remind us of the Constitution are hidden in the block below. Some words are hidden backward and some letters are used twice. See if you can find: CONSTITUTION, GOVERNMENT, NECESSARY, PROPER, ELASTIC, CLAUSE, POST OFFICE, LAWS, CONGRESS, BRANCH, ARTICLES, TAXES, SUGGESTED, POWERS, LISTED, ENUMERATED, LIMITATIONS.

```
S W A L I S T E D T A X E S Q
E N U M E R A T E D R B S U S
E S U A L C J P O W E R S G E
T N E M N R E V O G P A E G L
N E C E S S A R Y V O N R E C
E C I F F O T S O P R C G S I
C I T S A L E G K O P H N T T
S N O I T A T I M I L Z O E R
C O N S T I T U T I O N C D A
```

The Mini Page

By BETTY DEBNAM

More Big Ideas From Our Constitution

Checks and Balances

The word "check" has many meanings. One of them is to stop, or limit.

The term "checks and balances" means the limits put on each branch of government so that one branch cannot overpower another branch.

The writers of the Constitution "checked" the powers they gave each branch of government. The writers also wanted all three branches to limit, or "balance," each other's powers.

They thought checks and balances would make government safe and secure. They did not want one branch to threaten our freedom.

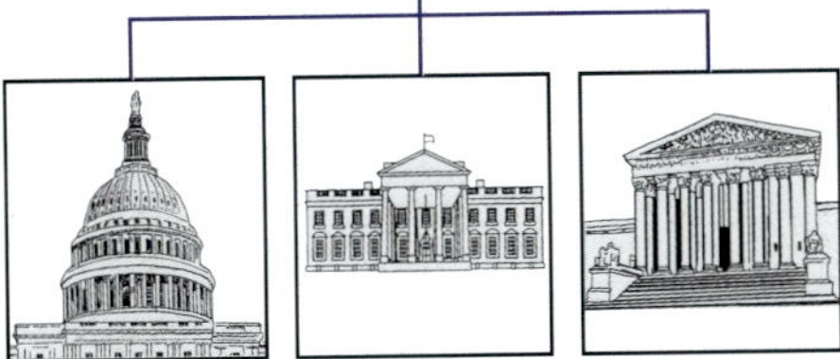

This mobile is a symbol of the balance of power. The government works well if the powers are balanced and checked.

We thank the staff of the National Archives and Lee Ann Potter, director of education and volunteer programs, for their help.

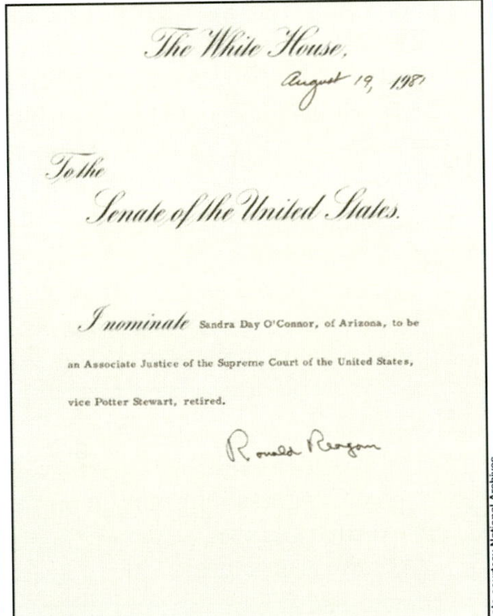

Checks and balances are easy to see in this 1981 letter from President Reagan (the executive branch) to the Senate (the legislative branch) about a Supreme Court justice (the judicial branch).

Laws

The Congress passes a law, but it can't become a law unless the president signs it.

The president can veto a law. Congress can override the veto by a two-thirds vote of both the Senate and the House.

The Supreme Court might declare the law unconstitutional.

Appointments

The president can appoint people to some important offices.

The Senate must approve the appointments.

War powers

The president is commander in chief of the armed forces.

Congress has the power to declare war.

Voting powers

The writers of the Constitution also checked the power of government by setting elections. Members of Congress and the president are elected for limited terms. If the voters want a change, they can go to the polls and vote officials out of office.

15

Page Three of the Constitution

The Constitution was handwritten on only four pages.

In this series, we look at this important document based on how the "articles," or sections, were presented page by page.

It's in the Constitution …
Page 3

1. Which role of the president described in Article II, Section 2, is shown in this photo?

2. What building is this? It is the place where lawyers and judges who know a lot about the Constitution and the law meet in Washington, D.C. It is mentioned in Article III, Section 1.

Answers: 1. the role of commander in chief. 2. the Supreme Court.

Page 3 of the Constitution includes most of Article II, all of Article III and the beginning of Article IV.

Article II is about the executive branch (the president). Article III is about the judicial branch (the Supreme Court). Article IV is about how the states relate to one another.

Article II
Section 1

The executive power shall be vested in a president:
- elected for a term of four years.
- there should also be a vice president chosen for the same term.

The section explains how the president and vice president will be elected. (This changed in 1804 with the 12th Amendment.)

The president will:
- be a natural-born citizen. • have lived in the United States for 14 years.
- be at least 35 years old.   If he dies, the vice president is the successor.

Section 2

Roles and responsibilities of the president:
- commander in chief.
- has the power to grant pardons.
- with the advice and consent of Congress, makes treaties, nominates Supreme Court justices and others.

Section 3

The president will:
- give Congress information on the state of the Union.
- execute all laws.
- commission officers.

Section 4

The president, vice president and all civil officers of the United States can be removed from office, or impeached and convicted, for treason, bribery and other crimes.

Article III
Section 1

Judicial power will rest in the Supreme Court and other courts.

Section 2

Establishes the jurisdiction of the cases that are to be considered by the court.

Section 3

Explains what the delegates meant by treason.

Article IV

Begins on Page 3 of the Constitution, but most of it is on Page 4. We will learn about that in the next issue in the series.

The President's Cabinet

The Cabinet is the name of a special group that gives the president advice.

The secretary of state works our agreements with other countries. 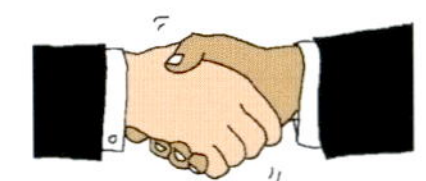

The secretary of the treasury supervises the collection of taxes.

The secretary of defense is in charge of the armed forces. 

The attorney general enforces the laws of the United States.

The secretary of the interior protects our natural resources and wildlife. 

The secretary of agriculture looks after the needs of farmers and our crops.

The secretary of commerce is interested in better U.S. business opportunities. 

The secretary of labor protects the interests of U.S. workers. 

The secretary of health and human services looks after our health and other needs. 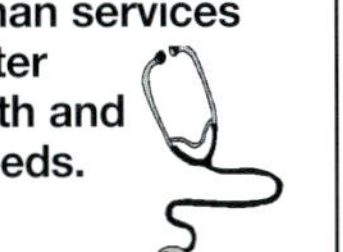

The secretary of housing and urban development works on housing and urban problems.

The secretary of transportation tries to set up better and safer ways to travel. 

The secretary of energy tries to solve our energy problems.

The secretary of education tries to gather information about and improve education.

The secretary of veterans affairs is concerned with the benefits of veterans and their families. 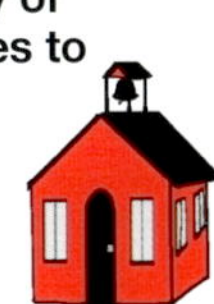

The secretary of homeland security works to make our country safer.

Other officials take part in Cabinet meetings. (The vice president also attends.)

The director of the Office of Management and Budget.

The U.S. trade representative.

The White House chief of staff.

Director of national drug control policy.

Head of the Environmental Protection Agency.

The president's Cabinet is not like the one you keep things in. The word "cabinet" comes from an old English word meaning a private meeting room. Most members have the title of "secretary." These people are in charge of big government departments. The Cabinet was not mentioned in the Constitution, but Article II, Section 2, gives the president the power to nominate members of the Supreme Court and "Others."

Mini Spy ...

Mini Spy and her friends are visiting the Supreme Court. See if you can find: • man in the moon • word MINI • ear of corn
• sailboat
• umbrella
• top hat
• ladder
• muffin
• pencil
• paper clip
• letter A
• letter D
• toothbrush
• letter W
• book
• cat

Basset Brown The News Hound's CONSTITUTION TRY 'N FIND

Words and names that remind us of the Constitution are hidden in the block below. Some words are hidden backward or diagonally, and some letters are used twice. See if you can find: GOVERNMENT, SUPREME, COURT, APPOINTMENTS, UNITED, STATES, TERM, PRESIDENT, CONSTITUTION, LAWS, TREASON, EXECUTIVE, JUDICIAL, BRANCH, CONGRESS, CHECKS, BALANCES, ARMED, FORCES.

```
J U D I C I A L A W S Q P M E
T R E A S O N K H C N A R B X
C H E C K S U P R E M E E A E
U N I T E D S E T A T S S L C
T R U O C O N G R E S S I A U
S E C R O F Y J A R M E D N T
A P P O I N T M E N T S E C I
G O V E R N M E N T O V N E V
N O I T U T I T S N O C T S E
```

The Mini Page®

By BETTY DEBNAM

Another Big Idea in Our Constitution

Federalism

As we have been learning in this series, the men who wrote our Constitution were very concerned about power. They knew that our country's first laws, the Articles of Confederation, did not give the national government enough power.

The Articles of Confederation were the laws that united the states together after the Revolution.

These articles had given too much power to the states.

In many ways, each state acted like a separate country. Strong national laws that were fair to everyone were needed to bind the country together.

The states had to give up some of their powers to the national government if the country was to survive. The writers of the Constitution set up what is called a "federal" system of government.

A federal system divides powers between the national government and the state governments.

As an American, you are a citizen of both the United States and the state in which you live.

We thank the staff of the National Archives and Lee Ann Potter, director of education and volunteer programs, for their help.

The division of powers in the federal system

This chart will give you an idea of how some of the powers are divided between the U.S. government and the states under the Constitution signed in 1787. Other limits were put on the U. S. government in the Bill of Rights of 1791.

The U.S. government

The U.S. Capitol in Washington, D.C. Our senators and representatives make national laws in this building.

Congress is given the power to:

- regulate (control) trade among the states and with foreign countries.
- declare war.

State governments

The California state capitol in Sacramento. California state senators and assembly members meet here to make the laws for that state.

State governments are given the power to:

- regulate trade within the state.
- set up marriage and divorce laws.

The United States and state governments

U.S. flag

California flag

- Both the U.S. and state governments are given the power to:
- collect taxes.
- borrow money.

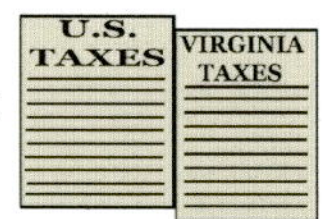

- take property for public use after paying a fair price.

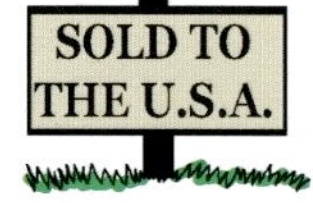

from The Mini Page by Betty Debnam © 2006 The Mini Page Publishing Company Inc.

Page Four of the Constitution

Our Constitution was hand-copied, or engrossed, on only four pages.

In our Mini Page series, we are looking at this important document based on how the "articles," or sections, are presented on each page.

It's in the Constitution … Page 4

Section 4 of Article 4 says that the United States must guarantee each state a "republican form of government." Congress decides if each state has a government that is republican, one that has members who are elected by the people.

Sometimes the head of the federal government, President Bush, meets with the head of a state government. Pictured here is Gov. Haley Barbour of Mississippi. They are discussing the damage caused by Hurricane Katrina in September 2005 with a manager of an oil refinery.

White House photo by Eric Draper

Site to see about the Constitution:
• **The National Archives at www.archives.gov**

Remember, our Constitution is only four pages long. The fourth page contains most of Article IV, and all of Articles V, VI and VII.

Article IV

Section 1

Contains the "full faith and credit" clause. It requires each state to respect the laws, records and court rulings of other states.

Section 2

Contains the "privileges and immunities" clause. It prohibits states from discriminating against citizens of other states.

This section also includes the "fugitive slave" clause, which was overturned by the 13th Amendment that abolished slavery.

Section 3

Provides for the admission of new states to the union.

Section 4

Says that the federal government will make sure that each state has institutions or lawmaking groups that represent the people.

Article V

Explains how the Constitution can be changed or amended.

Article VI

States that the Constitution and the laws of the United States are "the supreme law of the land."

Article VII

This article specifies that when nine of the original 13 states ratified (approved) the Constitution, it would go into effect.

The names of the signers of the Constitution are also on Page 4. We will learn more about them in the next issue.

★ ★ ★ ★ ★ **19** ★ ★ ★ ★ ★

Where Do the States Get Their Power?

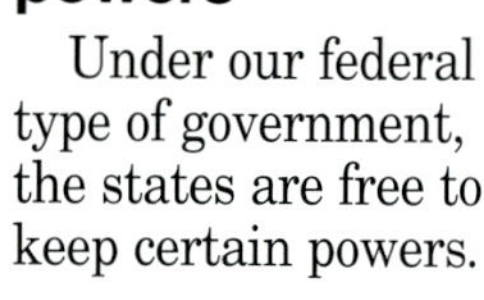

Reserved powers

Under our federal type of government, the states are free to keep certain powers.

Example: States have the power to set up a system to educate their people.

States have given some of their powers to local governments, but local governments are not mentioned in the Constitution.

To make certain that the national government did not get too much power, amendments, or changes, were added to the Constitution.

Example: The 10th Amendment makes it very clear that the powers not given to the national government are reserved, or saved, for the states.

Powers denied states

Some powers are denied to the states.

Example: In Article I, states are denied the right to print their own money and to make treaties with other governments.

The 14th Amendment denies the states the power to take away any of the rights granted a U.S. citizen.

What Federal and State Governments Cannot Do

The U.S. government cannot:

- take money out of the federal treasury unless given the power to do so by a law passed by Congress.
- grant titles of nobility.

Both the U.S. and state governments cannot:

- punish a person for breaking a law before it goes into effect.

State governments cannot:

- enter into treaties with other countries.

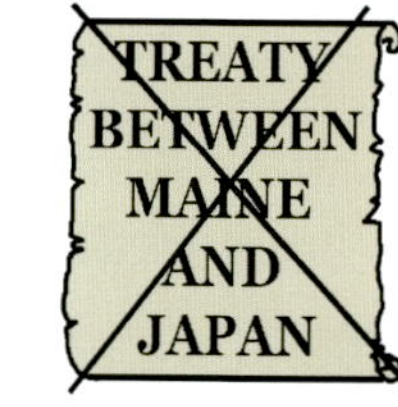

Mini Spy ...

Mini Spy and her friends are visiting the state capital of Albany, N.Y. See if you can find:

- ice cream cone
- two letter A's
- muffin
- paintbrush
- fish • book
- umbrella
- sailboat
- pencil
- squirrel
- number 3
- teapot • heart
- toothbrush
- word MINI
- typewriter
- caterpillar
- ear of corn
- letter W
- snake
- spoon

Basset Brown The News Hound's FEDERALISM

TRY 'N FIND

Words that remind us of state capitals are hidden in the block below. Some words are hidden backward or diagonally, and some letters are used twice. See if you can find: TOPEKA, HELENA, AUGUSTA, RICHMOND, TRENTON, TALLAHASSEE, LANSING, HONOLULU, RALEIGH, SACRAMENTO, MONTGOMERY, PHOENIX, BISMARCK, PROVIDENCE, INDIANAPOLIS.

```
B E C N E D I V O R P Z M V H
O W T J R A L E I G H T F E O
Q S A C R A M E N T O R L A N
M O N T G O M E R Y E E A T O
K C R A M S I B C K N N N S L
O R H E T O P E K A I T S U U
R I C H M O N D A Q X O I G L
E E S S A H A L L A T N N U U
I N D I A N A P O L I S G A X
```

The Mini Page®

Distributed by Universal Press Syndicate
© 2006 The Mini Page Publishing Company Inc.

By BETTY DEBNAM

from The Mini Page by Betty Debnam © 2006 The Mini Page Publishing Company Inc.

Sept. 17, 1787

Signing the Constitution

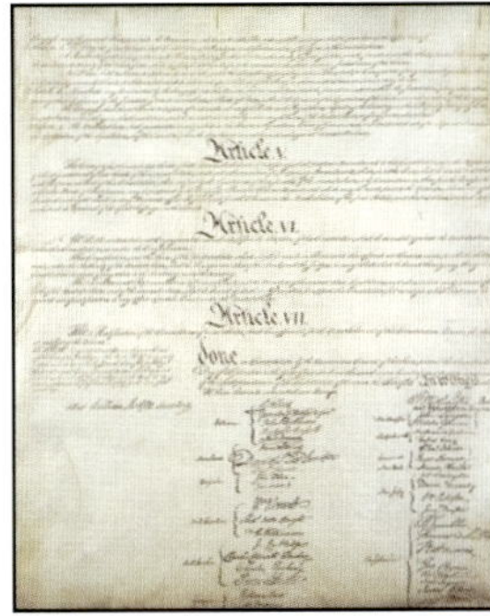
Page 4 of the Constitution.

Our Constitution's birthday is Sept. 17.

It was on that day in 1787 that the delegates to the Constitutional Convention in Philadelphia signed the document that they had worked on for nearly four months.

Franklin's speech

Ben Franklin was 81 years old. He did not have the strength to stand and make a speech at this meeting. He asked another delegate to read one he had written.

Benjamin Franklin

Franklin said that he did not agree with everything in the Constitution. However, he doubted that another convention would write a better one.

He urged all delegates to sign and support it.

We thank the staff of the National Archives and Lee Ann Potter, director of education and volunteer programs, for their help.

George Washington signed the Constitution first. Thirty-eight men signed in the order of their states, from north to south. (One delegate, George Reed, signed for John Dickinson, who was sick.) The 40th signature was that of Maj. William Jackson, the secretary of the convention. Above is a famous painting by the artist Howard Chandler Christy.

Not everyone signed

Some delegates would not or could not support the Constitution.

Three of the delegates at the final meeting refused to sign it.

George Mason of Virginia did not sign because it did not have a bill of rights.

Edmund Randolph, also of Virginia, thought that it gave the president too much power.

George Mason

Elbridge Gerry of Massachusetts thought it gave the central government too much power.

After it was signed

After the Constitution was signed, it became part of a six-page report that the convention sent to the Congress, which was meeting in New York City.

Congress received the package containing the Constitution, a resolution, and a letter from George Washington on Sept. 20, 1787. In less than a week, Congress considered it and sent it to the states for ratification, or approval. It was ratified by nine of the 13 states by July 1788.

George Washington

Signers of the Constitution

George Washington

George Washington was the most important man at the convention. He was such a great leader that his participation influenced others to take part. He did not take part in the debates during the sessions. However, he often consulted with members in committees and in private. He was unanimously chosen as the president of the convention.

George Washington

James Madison

James Madison is known as the father of our Constitution. He spoke out and worked very hard for a strong national government. The notes he kept are the best record of what went on.

James Madison

The signer's signatures are on the fourth, and last, page of the Constitution.

The convention that wrote the Constitution has been called the greatest meeting of wise men in history.

This mural of the Constitution's signers hangs in the rotunda of the National Archives in Washington, D.C., near the original Constitution. It was painted by Barry Faulkner in 1936 and is almost 14 feet tall and 35 feet long.

George Washington signed first. The other delegates signed from north to south.

Delaware
- George Read
- Gunning Bedford, Jun.
- John Dickinson
- Richard Bassett
- Jacob Broom

Maryland
- James McHenry
- Daniel of St. Thomas Jenifer
- Daniel Carroll

Virginia
- John Blair
- James Madison Jr.

North Carolina
- William Blount
- Richard Dobbs Spaight
- Hugh Williamson

South Carolina
- John Rutledge
- Charles Cotesworth Pinckney
- Charles Pinckney
- Pierce Butler

Georgia
- William Few
- Abraham Baldwin

New Hampshire
- John Langdon
- Nicholas Gilman

Massachusetts
- Nathaniel Gorham
- Rufus King

Connecticut
- William Samuel Johnson
- Roger Sherman

New York
- Alexander Hamilton

New Jersey
- William Livingston
- David Brearley
- William Paterson
- Jonathan Dayton

Pennsylvania
- Benjamin Franklin
- Thomas Mifflin
- Robert Morris
- George Clymer
- Thomas Fitzsimons
- Jared Ingersoll
- James Wilson
- Gouverneur Morris

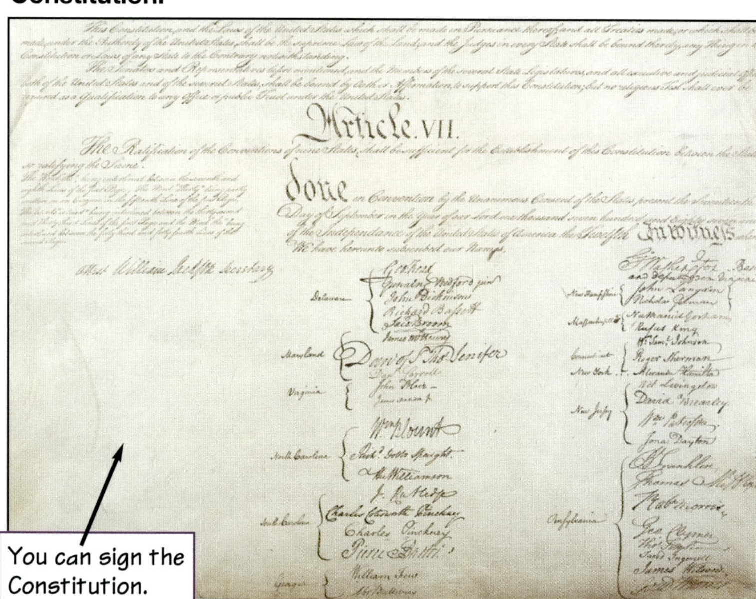

Site to see:
Biographies of the signers: http://www.archives.gov

The Convention Delegates

During the Constitutional Convention from May 25 to Sept. 17, 1787:

• 55 men attended at some time or other. Some went every day the convention was in session. Others came and went as they wished. Delegates from New Hampshire did not arrive until July 23.

• Four did not agree with what the convention was doing and left.

• 39 delegates, including George Washington, signed the Constitution. They signed in order, from north to south.

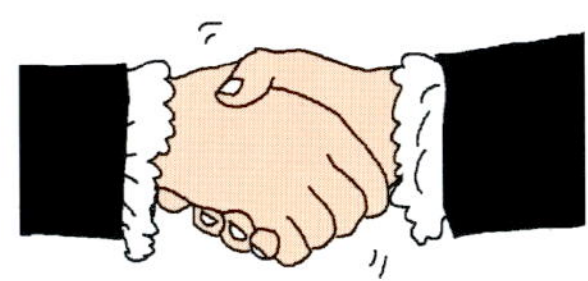

• Many of the delegates were old friends. The average age was 44. Ben Franklin was the oldest at 81. The youngest was Jonathan Dayton, 26, of New Jersey.

• Delegate John Dickinson of Delaware asked a fellow delegate to sign for him.

• In addition to the signatures of the delegates, William Jackson, the secretary of the convention, signed it. He had been an officer in the Revolutionary War, and later served as President Washington's private secretary.

• Almost all of the delegates had taken part in the government of the country or of their states. They knew firsthand about lawmaking.

• They were all well-educated for men of their time. Twenty-seven of them had graduated from college. All were readers of books, especially history books.

• Most (34) were lawyers. They were also planters, educators, ministers, doctors, merchants and soldiers. More than half had served in the Revolutionary War.

Mini Spy ...

Mini Spy and her friends are signing their copy of our Constitution. See if you can find: • exclamation mark

- ladder
- word MINI
- boat
- horse's head
- key • olive
- pencil
- bell
- mushroom
- fish
- kite
- number 3

Basset Brown The News Hound's

Constitution

TRY 'N FIND

Words and names that remind us of the signers of the Constitution are hidden in the block below. Some words are hidden backward or diagonally, and some letters are used twice. See if you can find: BEN, FRANKLIN, JAMES, MADISON, GEORGE, WASHINGTON, DELAWARE, NEW (twice), HAMPSHIRE, GEORGIA, NORTH, CAROLINA, PENNSYLVANIA, MASSACHUSETTS, YORK, MARYLAND, CONNECTICUT, VIRGINIA.

```
A I N A V L Y S N N E P F B F
C A R O L I N A E G R O E G R
J A M E S M A R Y L A N D E A
A I N I G R I V M A D I S O N
W A S H I N G T O N K Y O R K
S T T E S U H C A S S A M G L
D E L A W A R E V Z W E N I I
E R I H S P M A H T R O N A N
C O N N E C T I C U T Q N E W
```

The Mini Page®

By BETTY DEBNAM

from The Mini Page by Betty Debnam © 2006 The Mini Page Publishing Company Inc.

The First 10 Amendments to the Constitution

The Bill of Rights

The 1963 March on Washington for equal rights, led by Dr. Martin Luther King Jr., is an example of the right to peaceably assemble granted by the First Amendment.

photo courtesy D.C. Public Library

This girl was one of the thousands of marchers in the Washington march for equal rights in 1963.

photo courtesy National Archives

An amendment is a change or addition. The first 10 amendments to the Constitution are called the Bill of Rights. They were added in 1791 to limit the power of the national government over the people.

There were several reasons why a bill of rights was not part of the original Constitution. Many of the men who wrote the Constitution felt that another bill of rights was not needed because these rights were already protected by state constitutions.

Others felt that the Constitution says that all powers not given to the government go to the people. They thought that making a list of people's rights was not a good idea because they might leave one out.

We thank the staff of the National Archives and Lee Ann Potter, director of education and volunteer programs, for their help.

George Mason of Virginia was one of the delegates who thought that a bill of rights should be included.

In 1776, Mason had written the first bill of rights for the Virginia state constitution. Many other states copied his ideas. Mason refused to sign the U.S. Constitution because it did not have a bill of rights.

James Madison of Virginia realized that a bill of rights had to be added if the Constitution was to be accepted. Some states had agreed to sign only if this was done.

Madison was elected to serve as a representative to the first Congress under the new Constitution. He presented 17 amendments to Congress. These were cut down to 12.

On Oct. 2, 1789, President George Washington sent to the states a copy of these amendments for their approval.

By Dec. 15, 1791, enough states had approved 10 of the amendments so that the Bill of Rights went into effect.

The two amendments that were not adopted dealt with the salary of the members of Congress and a change in the number of members allotted to each state.

The First Amendment:
"Congress shall make no law respecting an establishment of religion, or prohibiting the free exercise thereof; or abridging the freedom of speech, or of the press; or the right of the people peaceably to assemble, and to petition the government for a redress of grievances."

The First Amendment of the Constitution is the best-known. In fewer than 50 words, it sets down many of our basic rights.

Mini Guide: The Bill of Rights

First Amendment

• **Freedom of religion** means that Congress cannot pass a law setting up a religion that everyone must follow. You are free to worship as you please.

• **Freedom of speech** means that you are free to speak out and give your side of things. Others are free to listen. However, there are some limits. You can't shout "fire" in a crowded room when there is no fire.

• **Freedom of the press** means that members of the press do not have to get what they are planning to print or say approved by the government beforehand. They are free to print what they wish as long as it is not a deliberate lie.

• **Freedom of assembly** means that you are free to meet peacefully.

• **Freedom of petition** means that you are free to ask the government to correct things that you think are wrong.

Site to see: The National Archives at www.archives.gov

The Mini Page is created and edited by
Betty Debnam

Associate Editors
Tali Denton
Lucy Lien

Staff Artist
Wendy Daley

Second Amendment

• **Guarantees the right to bear (carry) arms (weapons).** Congress cannot prevent people from owning guns for their own protection. However, states and local governments can make laws about who may own them.

Third Amendment

• **This amendment stops the government from forcing citizens to keep soldiers in their homes.** In Colonial times, citizens were forced to offer rooms to British soldiers.

Fourth Amendment

• **Limits searches and seizures.** This amendment says that before a police officer can enter your home, he must have a warrant, or legal paper from a judge, giving permission for a search or arrest.

Fifth Amendment

Grants the following rights:

• A person cannot be brought to trial for a serious crime until a grand jury, made up of a group of citizens, has studied the charges.

• If you have been tried for a crime, the government cannot bring you to trial again for the same crime.

• A person accused of a crime cannot be forced to say anything against himself (no self-incrimination).

• The government cannot take away your life or property, or put you in prison, without "due process of law."

• If the government has a good reason to take away your property for public use, it must pay you a fair price for that property.

Sixth Amendment

Lists the rights you have if you are charged with a crime. It guarantees:

• a speedy trial as soon as possible after your arrest.

• a fair jury of citizens who live in the same area where the crime was supposedly committed.

• a report of exactly what crime you are accused of.

• an opportunity to defend yourself against any witness who testifies against you.

• a lawyer to represent you, paid for by the government if you are unable to pay yourself.

Seventh Amendment

• **Extends your right to a trial by jury in civil cases** (those dealing with disagreements between two people or people and their governments). These are not punishable by death.

Eighth Amendment

• **The government cannot demand a person to pay bail or fines that are too high and unreasonable.** Also, punishment for a crime cannot be cruel or unusual.

Ninth Amendment

• **Entitles you to rights not listed in the Constitution.**

10th Amendment

• **Powers not given to the U.S. government are reserved to the states or to the people.**

Congress meets in New York City

The first Congress met in Federal Hall in New York City in 1789. According to the Constitution, there were 26 senators and 65 representatives. Federal Hall is no longer standing.

Why New York City?

The Bill of Rights document begins: "Congress of the United States begun and held at the City of New York on Wednesday, the fourth of March, one thousand seven hundred and eighty nine."

What was Congress doing in New York? New York City was then the capital of the United States. In 1790, Philadelphia became the capital, and then Washington, D.C., became the capital in 1800.

Celebrating Bill of Rights Day, Dec. 15

The original engrossed copy of the Bill of Rights hangs on display in the National Archives Building in Washington, D.C. It is so faded that it is hard to read.

photo courtesy National Archives

Ever since the year 1941, the president of the United States has issued a proclamation, or official announcement, that Dec. 15 is to be celebrated as Bill of Rights Day.

Bill of Rights Day

On Dec. 15, 1791, Virginia became the 11th state to ratify, or approve, the first 10 amendments to the Constitution. They became the law of the land.

One of the amendments that failed to pass dealt with the number of the members of the House of Representatives in Congress.

The other dealt with congressional pay raises.

An amendment dealing with raises was approved in 1992 by the addition of the 27th Amendment to the Constitution.

photo courtesy National Archives

When a citizen of one country has taken steps to become a citizen of another country, we say he or she is "naturalized." Many new U.S. citizens are naturalized on Bill of Rights Day at the National Archives building in Washington, D.C. The Bill of Rights is on display along with the Declaration of Independence and the Constitution.

Mini Spy ...

Mini Spy and Basset Brown are writing a petition for healthier school lunches. See if you can find: • man in the moon • peanut

- strawberry
- number 7
- exclamation mark
- kite
- hourglass
- carrot
- ruler
- question mark
- pencil
- fish
- sailboat
- arrow

Basset Brown The News Hound's

Bill of Rights

TRY 'N FIND

Words and names that remind us of the Bill of Rights are hidden in the block below. Some words are hidden backward or diagonally, and some letters are used twice. See if you can find: CONSTITUTION, ASSEMBLE, AMENDMENTS, JURY, APPROVAL, DELEGATES, BILL OF RIGHTS, GOVERNMENT, SPEECH, PRESS, POWERS, RELIGION, GEORGE, MASON, JAMES, MADISON, PETITION, TRIALS.

```
D G O V E R N M E N T Z H R G
P E T I T I O N O S A M C E E
B I L L O F R I G H T S E L O
P Y L E L A V O R P P A E I R
R R K O G M A D I S O N P G G
E U S E M A J P O W E R S I E
S J C N O I T U T I T S N O C
S T N E M D N E M A B V Z N X
A S S E M B L E S T R I A L S
```

By BETTY DEBNAM

from The Mini Page by Betty Debnam © 2006 The Mini Page Publishing Company Inc.

After the Bill of Rights

Amendments 11 Through 27

Ours is the oldest written, national constitution in the world. It has been changed only 27 times in more than 200 years.

The first 10 amendments to the Constitution, the Bill of Rights, were adopted in 1791.

Only 17 amendments have been added since then.

Two of these cancel each other out. The 18th, passed in 1919, brought in Prohibition, or a ban on the sale of alcohol. This was not a popular amendment. It was repealed, or canceled, by the 21st Amendment in 1933, 14 years later.

Civil rights amendments

The Bill of Rights and Amendments 13 and 14 are about our civil rights. Civil rights are those guaranteed to all citizens by the Constitution.

Government operations

Amendments 11, 12, 16, 17, 20, 22, 25 and 27 set up laws about how the government is to be run.

Voting rights amendments

Amendments 15, 19, 23, 24 and 26 are about voting rights.

We thank the staff of the National Archives and Lee Ann Potter, director of education and volunteer programs, for their help.

Women who fought for the right to vote were called "suffragists." They sometimes showed their support for their right to vote by marching in parades. The 19th Amendment enabled them to vote.

photo courtesy Library of Congress

Ways to amend the Constitution

Article V explains how the Constitution can be changed or amended.

An amendment can be proposed in two ways

• Congress can propose changes: Amendments can be proposed by a two-thirds vote of each house of Congress. All of our amendments have been proposed this way.

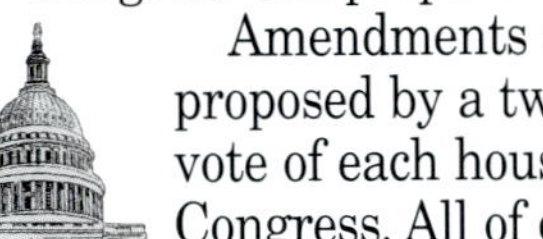

• States can propose changes: Two-thirds of the state legislatures, or lawmaking bodies, can ask Congress to call a national convention to propose an amendment.

An amendment can be ratified or approved in two ways

• Amendments become law when approved by the legislatures of three-fourths of the states. Twenty-six of the 27 amendments have been approved this way.

• Amendments become law when approved by conventions called by three-fourths of the states. Only the 21st Amendment, ending the ban on the sale of alcohol, was approved this way.

Mini Guide: Amendments 11-27

11th Amendment

• Gives rules for lawsuits against states. (1795)

This protects states against being sued in federal courts by citizens of other states or a foreign nation.

12th Amendment

• Creates a new way of selecting the president and vice president. (1804)

It states that electors are to cast two distinct votes: one for president and another for vice president.

13th Amendment

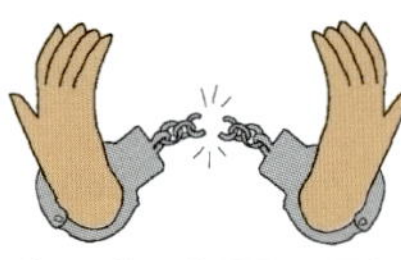

• Abolished slavery. (1865)

All slaves were freed at the end of the Civil War. This makes any form of slavery illegal.

14th Amendment

• Guarantees rights of citizenship, due process and equal protection under the law. (1868)

Today, all Americans, regardless of race, are protected by this amendment.

Next to the Bill of Rights, this is the most important amendment to protect the rights of all citizens.

Amendment 14 also defines who is a U. S. citizen. It says that all persons born or naturalized in the United States are citizens.

The amendment says, in part:

"Nor shall any state deprive any persons of life, liberty or property without due process of the laws."

The Supreme Court has used this amendment as the basis for a lot of the decisions granting equal rights.

15th Amendment

• Gives voting rights to former slaves. (1870)

Today, it protects the voting rights of all citizens regardless of race.

16th Amendment

• Gives the federal government the power to collect income taxes. (1913)

The government gets more money from this source than from any other.

17th Amendment

• Establishes election of senators by the people. (1913)

According to the original Constitution, U.S. senators were elected by state legislators.

18th Amendment

• Bans the manufacture, sale and transport of alcoholic beverages. (1919)

19th Amendment

• Gives women the right to vote. (1920)

In the early 1900s, some western states had already given women the right to vote.

20th Amendment

• Sets the dates of presidential and congressional terms. (1933)

21st Amendment

• Repeals the 18th Amendment, which had banned the manufacture, sale and transport of alcoholic beverages. (1933)

22nd Amendment

• Limits the president to two terms. (1951)

23rd Amendment

• Gives people in the District of Columbia the right to vote for the president. (1961)

24th Amendment

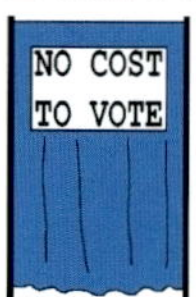

• Forbids having to pay a tax to vote in federal elections. (1964)

25th Amendment

• Establishes who would take charge if something were to happen to the president. (1967)

26th Amendment

• Lowers the voting age to 18. (1971)

27th Amendment

• Regulates the salaries of members of Congress. (1992)

The Mini Page is created and edited by
Betty Debnam

<u>Associate Editors</u>
Tali Denton
Lucy Lien

<u>Staff Artist</u>
Wendy Daley

23. These laws held our country together during the __________ _____ , but after the war, they did not work as well.

24. These laws did not allow the federal government to collect _______, regulate trade, or control the printing of money.

25. The men who wrote our Constitution made many compromises. One of them combined ideas presented in both the Virginia Plan and the New Jersey Plan and created two lawmaking groups, or "houses" of Congress. This became known as the _________ Compromise.

26. Another was known as the Three-Fifths Compromise, which concerned the number of representatives each state could send to the House of Representatives. Five ______ were counted as three "other persons."

27. Since representation in the House of Representatives is based upon population, the Constitution says that every 10 years a _________ of our nation's population will be taken.

28. According to Article I of the Constitution, members of the House of Representatives must be at least _____ years old.

29. According to Article I of the Constitution, members of the Senate must be at least ______ years old.

30. According to Article I of the Constitution, members of the House of Representatives are elected for ____ -year terms.

31. According to Article I of the Constitution, members of the Senate are elected for ___ -year terms.

32. Although Congress has the power to pass bills, they cannot become laws without the approval and signature of the _________.

33. According to Article II of the Constitution, the president must be at least ____ years old and must be a natural-born citizen.

34. According to Article II, the president is the _________ __ _______ of the armed forces.

35. The president is in charge of the executive branch of the government. Within the executive branch are other agencies that are led by members of the president's __________, whom he nominates.

36. According to Article II, the president has the power to grant pardons and nominate justices to the _________ __________.

37. Article V explains how the Constitution can be changed or ___________.

38. Article VII specifies that when ___ of the original 13 states ratified the Constitution, it would go into effect.

39. Our Constitution's birthday is September 17. It was on that day in 1787 that the delegates to the Constitutional Convention _____ the document.

40. The first 10 amendments to the Constitution are known as the _____ __ ______.

41. They were added to the Constitution in the year ______ to limit the power of the national government over the people.

42. The other _____ amendments address civil rights, government operations, and voting rights.

43. An amendment can be proposed in two ways: by ______ or by the states.

44. An amendment can be ratified in two ways: when approved by the _________ of three-fourths of the states, or by conventions called by three-fourths of the states.

Answers 

The page numbers indicate where the answers can be found.

1. government (p. 3)
2. Philadelphia (p. 3)
3. 1787 (p. 3)
4. four (p. 3)
5. National Archives (p. 3)
6. preamble (p. 4)
7. articles (p. 4)
8. 39 (p. 3)
9. amendments (p. 4)
10. parchment (p. 11)
11. James Madison (p. 22)
12. legislative (p. 4)
13. executive (p. 4)
14. judicial (p. 4)
15. three (p. 9)
16. together (p. 15)
17. enumerated (p. 12)
18. implied (p. 4)
19. state (p. 18)
20. we the people (p. 6)
21. George Washington (p. 6)
22. Articles of Confederation (p. 7)

23. American Revolution (p. 7)
24. taxes (p. 7)
25. Great (p. 9)
26. slaves (p. 9)
27. census (p. 10)
28. 25 (p. 10)
29. 30 (p. 10)
30. two (p. 10)
31. six (p. 10)
32. president (p. 15)
33. 35 (p. 16)
34. commander in chief (p. 16)
35. Cabinet (p. 17)
36. Supreme Court (p. 16)
37. amended (p. 19)
38. nine (p. 19)
39. signed (p. 21)
40. Bill of Rights (p. 24)
41. 1791 (p. 24)
42. 17 (p. 27)
43. Congress (p. 27)
44. legislatures (p. 27)